GUIDE TO NORSE PAGAN HOLIDAYS

UNLOCK THE ANCIENT MAGIC OF NORSE PAGAN HOLIDAYS

EMMA KARLSSON

FREE GIFT JUST FOR YOU

FREE 2023 NORSE GOD & GODDESSES CALENDAR
Use this link https://norsepaganwisdom.info/squeeze-
page1679502439646

OR

Scan the QR code below for your FREE Calendar NOW!

INTRODUCTION

I have always been a big believer in magic. I think that we take a lot of things for granted that are no less magical than they were a thousand years ago. Take memory, for instance. How amazing is it that we can recall something and have it play in front of our mind's eye while we're living in a completely different moment? Dreams—where do they come from? How is it that sometimes we can foresee the future in them?

And for those of us who do not have dreams and memories of the days of yore, we have these compact little dimensions of magic that line millions of shelves in libraries all over the world, these volumes of pages that can instantly make us hallucinate another time, another people, another tale. As Stephen King said, books are a uniquely portable magic.

Ever since I learned how to read, I've been portal-hopping into different times, learning about the legends of yesteryear and long-lost cultures.

I hoped to write such books one day and write two of them, I did. Both were about a subject that has long been near and dear to my heart. Ever since I was a little girl, I was fascinated by the stories of the Norse gods and goddesses, likening myself to Freya, she of the cats. I even had a makeshift chariot that I used to tether my cats to, hoping that they'd somehow transport me from my home in Kungsträdgården all the way to the past when gods like Odin and Thor oversaw the affairs of the Vikings when goddesses like Freya and Idunn blessed others with fertility and immortality.

Becoming a Norse Pagan and practicing paganism allowed me to bring that magic into my life by understanding Old Norse history, learning more about the gods, finding ways to venerate them, putting runes to work in my daily life, and understanding the mysticism of Norse magic.

And that is what it all comes back to—magic. Raw, unbridled magic.

In this book, I hope to help you unlock the ancient magic of Norse holidays, festivals, and celebrations, creating a splice in the space-time continuum to help you travel to a past of roaring fires over which boars were roasted, flagons filled with ales being drunk by hearty men with braided beards, brawny Vikings brandishing their battle-axes and calling for the All-Father's aid before diving headfirst into the ranks of their enemies, and practitioners of holy but dangerous magic performing rituals like seidr and spa to lift the veil from the future and peer into the possibilities of tomorrow.

Close your eyes. Imagine yourself standing at the cusp of a jet blue fjord, deep green hills all around you, the sky lumbering with heavy gray rainclouds, lightning flashing from behind those clouds, thunder rumbling deep in the vastness of the firmament, and those longships sailing down the fjord, carrying dozens of Norse warriors returning from a brave battle.

This is not just a vision. This is the memory of the world trying to make its way to you through these words. More than a thousand years ago, when myth was material, and the fibers of fables wove the fabric of reality, the Norse people lived fully actualized lives, had their daily routines, their customs passed through to them by their forefathers, and their celebrations to mark special occasions where mirth and merriment were called for.

That is where I'm taking you. Perhaps you shall see behind a tree the shapeshifter god of mischief, Loki, lurking, conspiring, thinking about how to take down Baldur. Maybe that grim bearded figure with the long cane is more than an old man in a busy marketplace. Notice his eyepatch and his intensity? Those ravens perched nearby? This could be the god of gods, Odin.

You are nearly there.

Step past the threshold and join the old gods and the old Norse people. Peer into their lives, learn how they used to brave hardships and celebrate their victories with flamboyant feasts while regaling each other with verses of skaldic poetry, and finally, become a part of them in spirit by celebrating those sacred days with a community of like-minded modern-day paganists who have revived the ancient magic, the same magic that shall now course through you.

Over the course of this book, we shall go over the Norse calendar, understand their division of the year into months, and see which celebrations and traditions they observed in which month. We shall take the pagan calendar and elucidate the festivals and sacred days within, starting with an overview and history of that particular holiday, the rituals followed in honor of that day, and related recipes and lore concerning that day.

Some prominent holidays observed by the Norse Pagans include Midsummer, Yule, and blóts which venerate Thor, Odin, Freya, the ancestors, and Valkyries. Different times of the year marked different celebrations depending upon occasions like harvesting, the heralding of summer, and to mark the end of the year.

After you've read this book, you will have an appreciation of the Norse culture and all it entails, including, in large part, the holidays, traditions, and various celebrations. You'll understand the importance of venerating the gods and goddesses through these rituals and festivals and learn how doing so can open a two-way communication channel that you can utilize to attain the gods' favor. Most importantly, you will be able to celebrate the Norse traditions like a true pagan.

A soft prerequisite for reading this book would be to understand the basics of Norse Paganism and Norse Mythology and know the lore of the gods and goddesses. Throughout this book, I will occasionally touch base with you and define words like blót, sumbel, seidr, and so on so that this book is inclusive for all readers. Wherever it is needed, I shall fill you in on the backstory of the Norse gods in context with the celebration.

So, without further ado, let us travel back in time to Scandinavia in the Viking Age.

Come, it's almost time for a feast and some good mead.

CHAPTER 1
THE NORSE CALENDAR

I f you asked someone their age back in ancient Norse times, they would tell you that they were a certain number of winters old. A child would say that he had lived through ten winters. This is just one of the characteristics of the Norse calendar, which was based on the seasons. The year was divided into months based on where the sun was in the sky, whether food was available or not, and the fertility of the land.

Scandinavia was home to some of the most extreme weather conditions, particularly in the winters. The year, reflecting that, was divided into summer and winter, both periods equally long.

Unlike how we celebrate New Year's, the Norse folk observed April 14th as the start of the new year, what with it being the first summer day as well.

The Norse calendar was considered lunisolar, utilizing both the sun's and moon's positions to mark days and months.

The modern Gregorian calendar follows an absolute chronology. For instance, this year is 2023 C.E. At any given time, a person can state absolutely that it's been x number of years, and the people would automatically understand their reference, making it easier to recall things in a uniform matter.

The Norse people, on the other hand, used relative chronology. They used to denote the number of years after certain important events. For instance, if there had been a great battle, they'd use that as a reference in time and say that it has been "two winters since that great Battle of Skellige."

It was not until the early 1100s that an Icelander named Ari "the Wise" Þorgilsson tried to get people to use absolute chronology.

Since it was a lunisolar calendar, the year was divided into phases of the moon, i.e. from full moon to full moon or new moon to new moon. Basing their division on moon sightings was not particularly accurate for the people, as nights in Scandinavia used to be quite bright, making it difficult to find the moon.

Picture it for a moment—the aurora borealis in all its cyano-green splendor dancing across the horizon, the rich tapestry of the Milky Way shining from on high, the lights from the stars shimmering in the sky. It's no wonder that the Norse Pagans held firmly to the belief that the sky was made from Ymir the giant's skull, and these stars were sparks captured from the fiery realm of Muspelheim, set into the dome-like jewels by the Gods Odin, Vili, and Ve.

THE DIVISION OF THE YEAR

The brightest period of the year, known also as the nightless time, was called Nóttleysa. Another interpretation of that word would be insomnia. These were the months we now know as May, June, July, August, September, and October. The time of the year these months coincide with was called sumar, as in summer. The sun was considered to be the bringer of warmth, light, and life. When it was high in the sky, that's when the Norse folk worked on their lands to grow crops.

The darkest period also called the period of short days, was known as Skammdegi. November, December, January, February, March, and April fall into the category of these vetur (winter) months.

The Old Icelandic calendar had its own names for the months and sometimes added a 13th month to make adjustments in the calendar. This month was called Silðemanuður, the Late Month. The Norse people also added four extra days in the middle of summer, calling them Sumarauki. As every month was 30 days long, these extra four days brought the day count of the year to 364, which is precisely 52 weeks. However, in leap years, instead of four days, seven extra days were added to Samarauki, making the year 53 weeks long.

The summer months were called Harpa, Skerpla, Sólmánuður, Heyannir, Tvímánuður, and Haustmánuður.

The winter months were called Gormánuður, Ýlir, Mörsugur, Þorri, Goa, and Einmánuður.

Each month in the Norse Calendar always started with the same day of the week.

SOLSTICES AND EQUINOXES

Solstices and equinoxes had a lot of importance in those days and affected the calendar, marked many of the celebrations, and were used as predictors for the arrival of different seasons as well. As Scandinavia was in the far north, these equinoxes and solstices were more noticeable there than anywhere else. For that reason, the equinoxes and solstices served as markers for significant celebrations such as blóts.

The Spring equinox served as a herald for Sumarmál, also known as the coming of summer. It marked the last days of the winter half of the year. Around this time, the food reserves of the people would have been running low, and they'd have desperately needed for summer to come. Sumarmál therefore served as a celebrative time to rejoice the end of hardship and for the arrival of ease. People used to move out from the confines of their homes, take in the daylight and the warmth of the sun, and schedule trading, travel, raiding, and feasting.

The Summer solstice marked Miðsumar (aka Midsummer). The Miðsumar blót has been noted in Snorri Sturlusson's sagas, stating that it lined with both the Norse religious beliefs and also with celebrating the bounties that summer brought.

The Autumn equinox served as the reminder that summer had ended and now winter had arrived. One of the most documented celebrations of this time of the year is

Vetrarnætr, Winter Nights. This time of the year coincided with the first winter month, which made it the ripe time to slaughter animals, salt and smoke them for the purpose of storing them for the winter ahead, and for stocking up their food reserves. This time of the year was also a popular time for weddings.

The Winter Solstice marked Miðvetr, Midwinter, which was a time for the Yule celebration. And yes, it's the same Yule that was later adopted by Christianity while still retaining many of its pagan rites. Originally, Yule was a celebration to mark the passing of winter. A blót was held to venerate the gods and ask for growth, good fortune, and bounties in the upcoming year. People would brew and drink Yule ale, gather around a roaring fire, and drink to their hearts' fill while cheering each other and venerating the gods.

THE CALENDAR MONTHS

Let us take a brief look at the Norse Calendar months before delving into them deeper in the upcoming chapters. The calendar was divided into two parts: Skammdegi, the winter months, and Nóttleysa, the summer months.

Skammdegi, also known as Vetur or Dark Days

Gormánuður (14th October to 13th November) Slaughtering Month

The first month of winter was called slaughtering month or butchering month. On the first day of this month, a winter blót was held to venerate Freyr and to thank him for his fertile bounties of the summer harvest. It's in this month that people start stocking up on animals and storing them for the upcoming months. That's how it got its name.

Ýlir (14th November to 13th December) Yule Month

This was the second winter month, also known as the Yule Month. The word Yule comes from one of Odin's names, Jólnir, which bore the word Jól. According to Norse Mythology, Odin traveled around Midgard and visited the locals. The kids used to fill their socks with hay for Odin's eight-legged steed, Sleipnir. In exchange, the white-bearded god would give them gifts in return. Sound familiar?

This month is also related to fertility and was a time that related to the cultivation of the earth.

Falling in winter, Ylir was also one of the darkest months. People spent most of their time indoors by the fire, eating the food they had harvested earlier that year.

Mörsugur (14th December to 12th January) Fat Sucking Month

During this month, the Norse folk provided nourishment to themselves by sucking on animal fat or bone marrow. Winter solstice is held this month, mostly on the 21st of December.

Some accounts differ, stating that the reason this month got its name was because the cold winters and short days literally sucked the light out of the people, making them resort to use candles made from tallows.

Þorri (13th January to 11th February) Frozen Snow Month

Þorri is the fourth winter month. It's when the Þorriablót is held. Women of the household invited Þorri, the winter spirit, into their house. This month was also a time when men were celebrated for their actions. They could choose a day for celebration, but warily. If the weather on that day was terrible, it was said to be a bad omen for the men.

Historically and traditionally, special dishes like sheep heads, rotten shark, meat jelly made from lamb's head, ram testicles, and other acquired taste delicacies were consumed during this time. Why? Because at this time of the year, the rations of the Norse people had run out of perishables. These hardier foods remained preserved for longer and provided the essential nutrients that the Norse folk needed to survive during this time.

Gói (12th February to 13th March) Sowing Month

The daughter of Þorri was known as Gói. The fifth month of winter was named after her and a blót was held in her honor. Additionally, this month was also considered women's month, just like the previous one was considered men's month. Men looked after their wives and celebrated women's achievements. It was also a time for planting the seeds for the incoming summer.

Einmánuður (14th March to 13th April) Lone Month

This month was dedicated to young boys. The month got its name because it was the last winter month. March 21st was considered to be the Vernal Equinox. On this day, a feast took place to celebrate fertility.

Nóttleysa, also known as Sumr or Nightless Days

Harpa (14th April to 13th May) Gaukmanadur

The first of the summer months, Harpa was dedicated to girls just like the three previous months were dedicated to men, women, and boys. The third biggest blót, also called the summer blót, was held this month to venerate Odin. This blót was meant to ensure victory in battles and wars, and happiness and tranquility in long travels.

Skerpla (14th May to 12th June)

Presumably named after a forgotten Norse deity, the second month of summer was considered the nesting season for birds. People in Iceland used to pick up those eggs for eating. It's interesting to note that it's considered illegal to do that nowadays in Iceland.

Another important facet of this month was the newborn lambs, who used to run free in the fields to suckle from their mothers. At night, the farmers used to milk the ewes in pens.

Sólmánuður (13th June to 12th July)

The summer solstice was observed in this month. It falls on the 21st of June these days. This month was named after the sun and was considered to be the lightest period in the entire year. Heads of households used to assemble and discuss political matters in this month, voting on different decisions. Given that it was the brightest time of the year, it was common for people to get married in this month.

Heyannir (13th July to 14th August) Hay Collecting Month

This month marked the midsummer. During this month, people used to gather hay, mow their grasses, water their plants, collect ferns, and stored fruit that couldn't bud.

Tvímánuður (15th August to 14th September) Corn Cutting Month

During this month, grain was harvested and corn was cut. Its name means the second to last month before winter. For the Norse people, harvesting was an important part of their designation, as this was dependent on the weather. They counted on the weather to be good so that they'd be able to harvest.

Haustmánuður (15th September to 13th October) Autumn Month

The last month of summer was also when the Autumnal Equinox was observed. Today, it falls on the 21st of September. This month was a reminder for people to be done with harvesting and get ready for the harsh winter months that lay ahead. Blóts for gods and goddesses like Sif, Thor, Gerdr, Freya, and Freyr were common during this month to thank them for the harvest and for providing people with the necessary means to survive the winter.

NORSE DAYS OF THE WEEK

The seven days of the week were named after different gods, except for Saturday, like so:

Monday — Manadagr (Moon Day)

The first day of the Norse week, Monday, was named after Mani, who had been punished to ride through the sky in his chariot forever. Mani had been named after a god who was considered way too brash. Mani was condemned to guide the course of the moon every night because of this. Mani is being pursued by a wolf who chases him across the horizon every night and ultimately catches him every night. And when that happens, the sun rises, and a new day begins.

Tuesday — Tysdagr (Tyr's Day)

Tyr, the OG god of war, patron of warriors, the lord of the sword, and the upholder of the law, was whom Tuesday was named after. It was agreed that if a war had to be started, the best day to do that was Tuesday.

Wednesday — Odinsdagr (Odin's Day)

Wednesday was named after the All-Father, the king of all the gods, the most powerful being in the Norse pantheon, the wisest of all deities, the diviner of mystical magic, and a patron of poetry.

Thursday — Þórsdagr (Thor's Day)

Thursday was named after Thor Odinson, the god of thunder and wielder of Mjolnir. When his chariot strode across the sky, thunder rumbled in the clouds, and lightning sparked from the wheels of the chariot.

Thursday was considered an excellent day for making decisions or holding meetings. This day, the day of the Midgard patron god, was also considered a very magical day.

Friday — Frjádagr (Freya or Frigg's Day)

Devoted to either Freya or Frigg, Friday was seen as a day to manifest the characteristics of the Norse goddesses—fertility, love, femininity, motherhood, and magic.

Saturday — Laugardagr (Laundry/Washing Day)

The Norse folk had set this day aside for taking baths and washing their clothes. It wasn't that they didn't take baths on other days of the week. It's just, Saturdays were sort of like their bath bomb, shower-gel, sit-back-in-the-tub-and-drink-wine kind of days.

The Norse folk, especially the Vikings, were famous for their hygiene. At one point, the English royalty, when they were being raided by the Vikings, became so afraid for their women, stating that the Vikings had such a rigorous hygiene routine—what with their braided and oiled hairs, their fresh smells, and their frequent bathing—that they were afraid their women would fall for them.

Sunday — Sunnudagr (Sun Day)

Sunday was named after Sol, Mani's sister, the goddess of the sun. Sol was also continuously being chased by a wolf who'd catch up with her at the end of every day, allowing her brother Mani to take to the skies and pull the moon.

Hopefully, by now, the Norse calendar, its associated days and months, and holidays are clear to you. Moving forward, we'll take a look at the major celebrations in each month and understand how they were celebrated, what sort of traditions were followed, and what each holiday signified.

CHAPTER 2
YULE

Yule remains one of the oldest pre-Christian Norse midwinter celebrations. The name is derived from the word hjol, which means wheel, serving to pinpoint the moment when the year's wheel is at the lowest point and is about to rise, as in the return of the sun from the wintery depths back into the sky. It's a harkening to summer, a time to wait for Baldur's return from the realm of Helheim. It is believed that upon his return, the winter grip on Midgard loosens, sending things back to their summer glory.

In 2023, it was celebrated on January 16-19. In 2024, it will begin on January 25 and will last three nights of the full moon.

The Icelandic sagas and other historical texts have given us descriptions of how Yule used to be celebrated. During this time, it was said that the veil between the living and the dead was at its thinnest.

Yule had 12 traditional days that began the festivities at the sunset of the winter solstice. And yes, you'd be right in connecting the dots. This, indeed, was a tradition stolen (alongside so many more others pertaining to Yule) in the name of Christmas and was distorted into what's now known as 12 days of Christmas.

The first night of Yule was a celebration for the Dísir and Frigga. It was called Mothernight. This night represented the rebirth of the world from this cavernous darkness back into the light. It was the shortest day of the year and the longest night. There was a vigil on this day, followed by a mothernight blót.

Odin, one of whose names is Jólnir (aka the Yule One), and all the other gods and goddesses were believed to be nearest to Earth at this time of the year. I almost feel forced to mention that the whole concept of Odin on Sleipnir descending upon Midgard and giving gifts and everything was also taken and morphed into the concept of Santa Claus.

Yule was also seen as the season during which the dead returned to earth and shared feasts with their beloved family members. Other creatures of fantasy, like elves, trolls, goblins, and fairies, also roamed around at this time of the year. They were either warded off for safety or had to be invited in for the sake of friendship and tranquility.

At this time of the year, Odin's horde of the dead rides most viciously. They can take you back to Hel if you cross their path. But it won't hurt if you put out food and drink for them, as the Wild Hunt isn't all evil. It can also come bearing gifts.

YULE CELEBRATIONS

Yule was celebrated by dancing, drinking, feasting, and hanging out with one's family. Some people used to burn sun wheels as part of the festivities going around. Some people used to swear oaths on holy boars. You read that right. There used to be boars that were hallowed for the sake of swearing oaths to. This particular thing survived in Swedish customs. They baked boar-shaped bread or carved blocks of wood shaped in the form of a boar and covered in pigskin for the purpose of Yule-oaths. Oh, and if that wasn't cute enough today, heathens bake boar-shaped cakes to make Yule-oaths to.

The more meaningful and promising of oaths and promises were taken during the feast or at the end of the sumbel. At the risk of sounding pedantic, here I'll note for the third time that the whole new year's resolution concept is a watered-down version of the Yule-oath.

As is the decoration of the house with fir or pine trees. That used to be a Germanic custom as well. The tree represented Yggdrasil. As is the Yule log, which was supposed to burn all night to symbolize the resilience of life and light in the face of cold and darkness. People used to use the ashes of the Yule log as amulets to wear for the rest of the year.

The 12 days of Yule were marked by making bread, cookies, cakes, and decorations. This is a custom that you can still put into practice during those twelve days. Each day was viewed as a miniature version of each month of the year.

Thor was also honored and venerated during Yule for driving back the frost giants. As was Frey, for giving us fertility and prosperity in the past year and the upcoming year. Odin was revered as the god of all and the leader of the Wild Hunt.

CELEBRATING YULE LIKE A PAGAN

You can get started with the simplest and most convenient tradition. Bring a fir or pine tree and decorate it. At its core, this remains a pagan tradition. The tree here represents the Yggdrasil—something that many religions have tried to emulate.

A Yule log is another great way to celebrate Yule. You can find a great oak log and set it ablaze in your fireplace or as a bonfire. You can use its ashes to use for lighting next year's log.

Next up, you can host two different Yule blóts if you're in the mood for festivities. One can be a Mothernight blót in honor of Frigg, and the other can be a Midwinter night blót in honor of Thor.

Any oath that you swear on Yule is considered unbreakable according to pagan law. So, whatever oaths you do make during the feast, sumbel, or drinking, you have to be very mindful of your words because the gods are watching.

Besides the Yule feasting, blóts, and offerings, one last important part of the celebrations was brewing ale and drinking it. If you're not particularly fond of making your own mead, there's always store-bought mead that you can drink to commemorate this special celebration.

Oh, and one last thing. Yule was a time for giving gifts. The Norse people were big on giving gifts to each other, and this was especially observed during Yule.

CHAPTER 3
YULE RECIPES

KRANSEKAKE

A TRADITIONAL SCANDINAVIAN YULE DESSERT IS KRANSEKAKE, A RING-SHAPED CAKE MADE OF SEVERAL CONCENTRIC RINGS OF ALMOND CAKE AND TOPPED WITH WHITE ICING AND SUGAR-COATED ALMONDS.

INGREDIENTS

Dough

- 8 ounces (2 cups) sliced blanched almonds
- 3 cups confectioners' sugar
- ½ teaspoon coarse salt
- 2 large egg whites
- Unsalted butter, softened, for molds

Icing

- 1 pound confectioners' sugar
- 3 large egg whites or five tablespoons meringue powder mixed with ½ cup water
- Paste or gel food coloring (optional)

DIRECTIONS

1. Grind almonds with a grinder or food processor
2. In a bowl, mix in almonds just ground with sugar. Once mixed well, add in the two egg whites and mix. (There will be a point when using your hands to mix makes sense because of the texture of the dough.) Once it gets like this, put a piece of plastic wrap on top and place it in the fridge for at least 3 hours
3. Now that it's cold, the dough will be easier to mold. Roll the dough until it becomes one finger thick, about a ½ inch.
4. Preheat the oven to 200C
5. You use molds or draw rings out on a piece of parchment paper. Make 18 rings of the right size so they can rest on each other. Once you place the dough rings in molds or on parchment paper - put them in the fridge for 15 minutes to harden (8-10 min middle shelf)
6. Make icing:
   a. Combine confectioners' sugar and egg whites in the bowl or in an electric mixer fitted with the paddle attachment). Mix on medium-high speed until combined and thickened, about 8 minutes
   b. If decorating with more than one color, divide the icing into batches. Using the end of a toothpick, add food coloring until the desired shade is achieved
7. Assemble rings to make a tower. Use the icing to help them stick together
8. Serve and enjoy!

POLKAGRISKOLA
SWEDISH PEPPERMINT CARAMELS

INGREDIENTS

- •4ounces hard peppermint candies
- 1 ³⁄₄cups heavy cream
- 1cup superfine sugar
- 6tablespoons golden syrup (British) or 6 tablespoons dark corn syrup
- 3tablespoons honey
- 7tablespoons unsalted butter

DIRECTIONS

- Put the peppermint candies into a plastic bag and crush them coarsely with the flat side of a meat mallet. Using a large sieve, sift candy pieces, discarding fine powder; set candy pieces aside.
- Line the bottom of an 8"x8" baking pan with parchment paper; grease parchment paper with nonstick cooking spray and set aside.
- Heat cream, sugar, syrup, and honey in a 6-inch diameter 2-quart saucepan over medium heat; stir until sugar dissolves, about 5 minutes. Bring to a boil and attach a candy thermometer to the side of the pan; cook, without stirring, until mixture reaches 250 F, about 45 minutes. Remove pan from the heat and add butter. Using a wooden spoon, stir until smooth, about 3 minutes.
- Pour toffee mixture onto prepared baking pan and sprinkle evening with peppermint candy peices, pressing them lightly into toffee with the back of a spatula. Let cool completely; cut into 64 squares to serve.

Enjoy!

CHAPTER 4
DISABLÓT

D isablót is a pagan festival that honors the Norse goddesses, spirits, and ancestors. Collectively, the latter two are called Dísir. The word itself is a concatenation of Dísir and blót.

As a festival, disablót was more associated with harvesting. Like Sígrblót, this was held in a very private manner within one's house as a way to honor one's female ancestors and the female goddesses and spirits that looked over one's family.

That being said, there was not exactly a specific day for this sacrificial holiday. It could have been held during winter nights. Some accounts state that it took place at the beginning of February.

HOW WAS DISABLÓT CELEBRATED

Historically, it was a day for venerating one's female ancestors and deities. The people did this by setting up alters and setting out offerings of their favorite drinks, food, and tokens. It was a time when female deities like Freya, Frigg, Skadi, and Sif were invoked so that they'd look over the people and grant their favor. It wasn't just reserved for the deities. The Norns, as in the sisters who shaped the fate of everything, were also venerated during this time, as were the Valkyries, spirits who took the fallen soldiers to Valhalla.

The blót was very family oriented, from what we can tell from the historical sagas. As it was family-focused, both old pagans and modern heathens today observe some part of this in the privacy of their homes.

The disablót was described in Olaf Hraldsson's saga as:

> *"In Sweden there was an age-old custom whilst they were still heathen that there should be a blood offering in Uppsala during Góa-month. Then they would sacrifice for peace and victory for their king. And thither would they come from all over Sweden. There also were all the Swedish things. There was besides a market and a fair, and it lasted a week. But when Christianity came to Sweden they still kept the law thing and the market there. And when Christianity prevailed throughout Sweden and the kings no longer sat in Uppsala, the market was shifted and held at Candlemas. It has always been held then ever since, but now it does not last more than three days."*

In the Ynglinga saga, it was said:

> *"King Adils was at a sacrifice to the goddesses (Dísir) and rode on his horse around the temple; the horse stumbled under him and fell; so the king also rolled over, and his head fell against a stone, so that his skull burst and his brains lay on the stone.*

That was his death; he died in Uppsala and there is now his howe. The Swedes called him a mighty king."

The other traditional part of this blót was called charming the plow. It was when farming equipment, seeds, and the farming fields were blessed and charmed so that they'd grow plenty of harvest during the summer.

HOW YOU CAN CELEBRATE DISABLÓT

This is a day for all the women in your life, not just your wives and partners. It can serve as a day where you appreciate your mother, aunts, sisters, and daughters. There's a certain divinity in femininity, especially within Norse Paganism. From the magical rite of giving birth to the transcendental duty of bringing the brave dead to Valhalla, there have been various ethereal acts that women have done in Norse Mythology.

Frigg, the mother of Baldur, did everything she could to ensure that her son would be unharmed by every single being in the world. She took an oath from every single creature and unliving thing as well so that they would not harm her son. That is just one example from hundreds where deities of Norse Mythology have shown their quality.

You can venerate individual female deities today, such as:

- Freya for fertility
- Idun for her fruitful bounties
- Eir for growth, nurturing, and healing
- Frigg, for courage, hearth, and wisdom
- Sif for sustenance

You can light a candle at your altar for your female ancestors and the goddesses. If there's a feast or a gathering at
your house for this blót, share stories of the women in
your life, tell the remarkable tales of the goddesses and the
dísir. Did your loved ones leave any recipes? Perhaps
some special recipe for chicken pot pie by your grand-
mother or the perfect brisket by your nana? It can be an
excellent time to cook such a meal and offer some of that
food with some wine to your female forebears.

If you're in the mood, there's always a bonfire that you can
light to sit around, drink, and share stories of your female
ancestors.

Pray to the dísir. They're listening to you. You've held this
blót in their honor. Now you have their ear. Ask for help.
Seek their counsel for whatever troubles you're facing. You
can pray for protection on your life's journey.

Lastly, you can keep the dísir in your mind and do something that would make the goddesses, the Dísir, and your
ancestors proud.

CHAPTER 5
ÞORRABLÓT

This Norse festival used to take place in the month of Þorri, which, as we saw from the first chapter, took place between January and February. This year, in 2023, it was celebrated from January 20th to February 18th. If you'd put yourself in the shoes of the Norse folk, you can imagine how they must have felt by then, what with being smack in the middle of winter. It must have been tiring for them to brave through that harsh weather without many resources. And as we'll see in this chapter, the resources that they did have were very harsh in nature.

WHAT WAS ÞORRABLÓT?

Today, Þorrablót is still celebrated in Iceland as a cultural celebration. For Norse Pagans, this is a time to celebrate the winter spirit Þorri.

Þorrablót was seen as a midwinter sacrificial celebration wherein offerings were made to Þorri and the Norse gods.

After the Christianization of Scandinavia, it was abolished, with its traces just left in historical texts. But old roots run deep, and if given time, they resurface, just like Þorrablót resurfaced late in the 19ᵗʰ century, and it is still being celebrated by pagans all over the world.

Simply put, like other blóts, this blót was considered a sacramental feast. Þorri was seen as this personification of the Scandinavian winter, often depicted as being brute, merciless, and cold. In the Orkneyinga saga, Þorri (his name literally meaning "frost") was said to be a Finnish King to whom early offerings were made at midwinter.

Other sources state that this blót was in honor of Thor. But there's a disagreement between both theories. Some say that Thor and Þorri are one and the same and that Þorri is just the post-Christian version of Thor.

The celebration of Þorrablót comes at the start of Bóndadagur, a day reserved for celebrating husbands, and ends with Konudagur, a day for celebrating women or wives.

As for why it was celebrated, the historical consensus is that it was meant to be this reinforcing event where people would bolster their spirits with traditional food, give each other the encouragement they needed, and acknowledge and venerate Þorri, letting him know that the Norse folk's spirits had not died down in this winter and that they acknowledged the fact that he was a necessary force of nature, and not something vile. And if this celebration was meant for Thor, it was because he protected Midgard folk from the Rime-Thurses, aka the frost giants, in those vulnerable winter months.

Þorrablót was also celebrated to await the arrival of summer.

As with any blót, the celebration included copious amounts of alcohol and meats. But these meats and delicacies differed from the regular menu at other blóts.

Interestingly enough, the weird selection of food was one of the factors that caused this celebration to be revived in Reykjavik in the 1950s when a restaurant started offering food that was exclusive to the Icelandic countryside.

HOW WAS IT CELEBRATED?

With lots and lots of bizarre cuisine, that's how. And for good reason. With the blót taking place in the middle of winter, people used to come together in each other's houses for drinking, eating, roasting, toasting, and loads of merriment. Traditionally, this was a time not for plundering, pillaging, raiding, or hunting; this was a time to sit by the fire, be with one's family, and survive through the cold and dark days of winter.

Because of the timing of this blót, much in the way of food was not available, with the only available food being pickled and smoked produce left over from the previous year.

What kind of produce? Well, there was rotten shark's meat, congealed sheep's blood in a ram's stomach, boiled sheep's head, blood pudding, sour ram's testicles, liver-suet sausage, headcheese, and whale blubber.

After eating this food, it was washed down with strong alcohol. In modern times, Brennivin, also known as Icelandic schnapps, is drunk after all that food.

The reason for this peculiar assortment of food was because these parts of the animals were tough, didn't rot or decay or soften as much, and were hardy enough to survive through the winter, although they were preserved in fermented whey. This fermented whey is used to break down the proteins in the food, making it tender and more easily palatable.

Another reason for this strange buffet was that the Norse folk utilized all parts of an animal, especially in winter, wasting nothing. That's why body parts like the stomach, head, testicles, brain, and intestines were used.

HOW YOU CAN CELEBRATE IT

If you are a vegetarian or are averse to the strong afore-mentioned seafood, you can avoid the meats in favor of vegetables, bread, or other favorable food while remembering the spirit of this celebration.

It's about being close to your family in tough times. Back in those days, winter was no laughing matter. The Norse folk did not have the same luxuries that we do, which meant that the mortality rate was quite high. But they did not let their hardships deter them; rather, they found purpose in these hardships, celebrated the fact that they braved them, and became closer to one another.

You can host a dinner for your friends and family, followed by a round or two of drinks. After that, how about an intimate sumbel where you and your friends and family can venerate the gods and remember the ancestors? There can be singing, dancing, telling tales, playing group games, and whatever way of merriment suits you best.

Back in the old days, Þorrablót used to be a very lively affair with performances, singing, poetry reading, and dancing. If you're in the mood for something more festive than a home dinner, how about assembling with fellow neo-pagans to celebrate Þorrablót with a communal spirit?

More than any other celebration, Þorrablót was one where traditional cuisine came into play and continues to be an important part of the festival. It's an example of how history, culture, and creed can be preserved in forms other than written and spoken; it can also be stored in food.

CHAPTER 6
BÓNDADAGUR AND KONUDAGUR

The months of Þorri and Góa had celebrations for men and women respectively. The men's version —or husband's day—was called Bóndadagur and the women's version was called Konudagur.

In the modern calendar, Bóndadagur falls on the 21st of January and Konudagur falls on the 18th of February.

BÓNDADAGUR

On this day, the men of the house were treated, celebrated, and pampered.

On the morning of Bóndadagur, the man was supposed to go out of his house dressed in just a shirt, with one leg of his trouser dragging the other one behind. While hopping on one leg, the man would go and hop from house to house, rousing other men and greeting Þorri.

On this day, the man's wife was supposed to take more care of him than usual, offering him the delicacies of the season, spending time with him, and indulging him. For the women, it was a chance to show their appreciation for all that the men had done over the year. Women were also known to give their men presents or gifts, particularly something that related to their profession.

Because of their vicinity, Þorrablót and Bóndadagur have had similar themes in the past, especially when it comes to food. In the old days, the only cuisine available to the Norse folk during this time was hardy, fermented food like ram testicles, lamb's head, blood sausage, dried fish, and blubber.

The revival of this day has seen new traditions in Iceland, where instead of offering their men the aforementioned foods, women prepare more traditional dishes, take their men out on a date, and buy them presents. Still, some tradition has managed to seep into the modern version of man's day. Women in Iceland cook smoked lamb called hangikjot for their men.

This was often seen as a time for reciprocity. The men appreciated what their women did for them, and made sure to pay it back the next month on Women's Day or Konudagur.

Traditionally, this was a day when men flaunted themselves in feats of strength. After a feast, the men would get together and playfully fight with each other, participate in tug-of-war competitions, and race each other around the commune.

If you're wondering how you can celebrate this day (as a female), plan a special day for the special man in your life. It does not have to conform to something traditional. Most men are very individualistic when it comes to preferences. Perhaps your partner is an introvert who does not like going out and partying as much as he likes sitting by the fire, reading a book, or watching a movie with you.

A nice way to celebrate this day would be to make him a meal that he likes. If he likes hanging out with his friends, have him do that. Maybe invite all of his friends over to catch a game on the TV.

KONUDAGUR

Women's Day, or konudagur, was celebrated in Góa. Góa was the daughter of Þorri and the great-grandaughter of Frosti. Once upon a time, she took a fancy to a boy during Þorrablót and ran away with him. Her father was so worried about her that he sacrificed to the gods to find out where his daughter had gone. That sacrifice took on the name of Góublót.

In that spirit, konudagur used to be celebrated. It was a time when the women of the house were appreciated by the men. Their husbands used to bring them flowers, gifts, and trinkets. For the men, this was an opportunity to pay back the affection that they had received a month ago on Men's Day.

For the men, this was also a time to show appreciation towards the female goddesses, especially those who had to do with fertility and motherhood. They paid their respects to Frigg and Freya, who were considered goddesses of marriage, domesticity, motherhood, fertility, and love. As this was considered a blót, there was a traditional feast followed by drinking and toasting. The toasting, in this particular case, was for women and their feats throughout the year. Braving the winters was not just the man's business in the old days. The women had just as much responsibility during that time, from raising little children in the cold to providing hot meals to everyone in the house and so much more.

As a pagan, you can celebrate konudagur with your wife, girlfriend, or partner in the following ways:

- Learn about the history of the old Norse goddesses. It's a time for us to learn to be appreciative of the feminine side of divinity and how it manifests in the women around us.
- Treat your lady to a great night out, be there for her in ways that she wants, listen to her, and make her feel appreciated by giving her thoughtful presents.
- Become a part of the conversation about women's rights and gender equity and take the necessary steps to be an ally to those who are experiencing human rights hardships under the name of feminism.

If you're a woman, this can be a day:

- To treat yourself. Visiting a spa wouldn't exactly be out of tradition. Back in the olden days, women used to visit Icelandic hot water springs for a relaxing bath.
- To invite all your lady friends and host a gathering. Again, this is a very traditional thing that the women of yore used to do. They'd get

together for lunch, spill some Norse tea, and connect with each other as well as the goddesses. Getting together with other women can be a great way of harnessing female energy, reenergizing yourself, and reminding yourself of the resolve that you possess, that the legends of old such as the shieldmaidens and Valkyries possessed, and that the goddesses, benevolent and caring that they are, are looking over you.

CHAPTER 7
SÍGRBLÓT

S ummer was now upon the Norse folk, and for them, this meant one thing—victory! They had braved through the sheer winter and had come out on the other side alive, jubilant, and their spirits undeterred. This holiday fell on the fourth full moon after the winter solstice. This year, it was held on April 6th.

WHAT IS SÍGRBLÓT?

In the Ynglinga saga, Odin proposed three holidays:

"There should be sacrifice towards winter for a good year, and in the middle of winter for a good crop, and a third in summer, that is the victory sacrifice."

The three holidays that Odin was referring to were Winter Nights, Yule, and Sígrblót.

This celebration was carried out in Odin's name and was dedicated to victory in war, good fortune on raids, and pleasant journeys. In his book about Norse Mythology,

John Lindow wrote that the summer ceremony was all about victory, not just in terms of post-winter victory, but a victory of every sort. Now that winter was over, the Vikings were getting ready to go on long journeys, prepare for battles, and make plans for raids. The departure of ships, the planning of attacks, and everything else came at a time when Sígrblót was being celebrated.

There's an interconnectedness between Sígrblót and the summer months. The last five days of the winter half of the year were called Sumarmál, which meant the summer portion. They were also known as Sumarnætr, meaning summer nights. Just like winter nights. Just as the Alfablót and Disablót were held during Vetrnætr, Sígrblót was celebrated during the Sumarnætr.

We cannot fully understand how important this time of the year was for our ancestors. Nature was being reborn, the trees got their leaves back, flowers started blossoming in the meadows, and the ice that had frozen over the lakes and bays started thawing, making it possible for the Vikings to move beyond their farmsteads.

If I may give a brief and relevant example, imagine the lockdown that we all had to collectively face during the Covid outbreak. We weren't able to get out of our houses, weren't able to socialize with friends and family members, and, more importantly, were kept from doing things that were important to us, such as our jobs. It was a time when we were all literally bound to our houses.

For the Norse folk, it was like that but worse. There was also the brutal cold, the lack of resources, and on top of that, no infrastructure of healthcare that could see them through their winter-borne diseases. It didn't last for a few weeks. It lasted for half the calendar year, this tempestuous time.

To come out of that, unscathed and alive, was cause enough for them to celebrate with each other. And that's why they celebrated Sígrblót with as much fervor as they did.

It was at this time of the year that the Norse folk saw the splendor of Freyr, Odin, and Baldur. Freyr blessed the people with summer bounties, made sure that the lands were fertile, and allowed the farmers to plant their crops so that they'd be ready for the upcoming months. Odin, by dint of his being a warrior god, saw over the affairs of the warriors and the fighters and bode them strength in their battles to come. The god of sunlight and splendor, Baldur, radiated his light everywhere, thawing the ice, nourishing the crops, and ensuring that the beauty of summer redeemed itself from the icy grip of winter.

HOW CAN I CELEBRATE IT?

One of the more profound ways in which we can get in touch with our ancestral roots is by putting ourselves in their shoes. Imagine yourself a Norse pagan in ancient Scandinavia. Now try to bring up the same feelings as a Norsemen would at the time of Sígrblót. They are happy that they can now see the sun in all its summer splendor. They want to greet the sun. So should you. Sígrblót is a three-day celebration that starts on the first Sun. Historically, people used to go and greet the sun by watching the first sunrise. They also happened to have warm drinks in hand.

You can do the same. Go with your friends or family, preferably after drinking an energizing warm beverage, and then go on a hike or a walk along the beach or in an open park. Here, you'll get your first sighting of the summer sun, and it should be a magnificent one. By Odin's beard, this is the same sun that your ancestors beheld all those thousands of years ago. And it is the same sun that you are witnessing.

A blót would not be complete without giving your offering to the gods. Remember Freyr, Freya, Odin, and Baldur during this particular blót. While traditionally, they used to offer animals and blood offerings, we understand that being a modern pagan means that some of the traditions have to be brought up to the times. Instead of meat or blood, think about making sacrifices at a makeshift altar, sacrifices containing wine, mead, or any special token that the aforementioned gods and goddesses loved.

Odin loved his ravens. Perhaps some raven feathers would be a good tribute for him?

Freyr loved his enchanted ship given to him by the dwarves. He also had a thing for boars. He'd certainly appreciate a maritime gift, perhaps one of those tiny ships in a bottle? You are allowed to be as creative as you desire.

Freya had a thing for cats (as don't we all?), and Baldur had a thing for beauty. Are you picking up what I'm laying down?

An offering was usually made by placing it at an altar and then verbally letting the god know that it was for them and for what purpose.

A blót would also not be considered complete without a blót feast. Your ancestors celebrated this particular day with a warm spirit. You can also enjoy a grand feast with your family. Heck, if the modern religions can have their Easters and Christmases and Thanksgivings, we can have our Winter nights, Yule, and Sígrblót!

You can close off this blót with a round of sumbel. It's when everyone gathers around, passes a flagon or horn of mead, and toasts the gods, the ancestors, and the legends of yore. It's also the right time to share your stories with others and listen to their tales.

Lastly, Sígrblót is a wonderful time to set goals for the summer. It was a time when victory was sought from the gods. You can also seek victory for the goals that you set.

CHAPTER 8
MIDSUMMER

With its celebrations synonymous with Sweden, Norway, Finland, and Denmark, where it is observed as a national holiday, the festivities of Midsummer fall between the 19th of June to the 25th. It was a time to celebrate one's connectedness to the summer side of nature, the light, warmth, greenery, and fertility of the land. The pagans celebrated this occasion as a victory of light against dark, and thanked the gods and goddesses (namely Freyr, Freya, and Baldur) for the joys of summer. It was an occasion marked by bonfires, diverse foods, and rituals to ward off evil spirits. As this was the longest day in the year and the shortest night, this was the perfect time for such rituals.

They would light these huge bonfires to ward off darkness and all the bad forces that it contained. Plants were another magical aspect of this celebration. The utilization of green magic for attaining powers during the summer solstice was one of the reasons why women placed flowers and herbs under pillows on the eve of Midsummer.

It's a holiday that has retained its authenticity to this day and is celebrated wholeheartedly in Scandinavia. This year, in 2023, it's going to be celebrated on the 24th of June.

WHY WAS MIDSUMMER CELEBRATED?

Midsummer was a time to pray for abundance in the harvest. The harvest in question was not just that coming from crops and farming. Fertility, especially in women, was celebrated, and those who had been newlywed were honored and prayed for so that they'd have good offspring. It was a time to celebrate the serenity of nature, something that the Norse folk had very little of during the winters.

The Swedes, Finnish, and Danish all celebrate it in their unique ways.

The people of Sweden often moved to greener pastures during this holiday to celebrate in nature. For them, the Midsummer festivities began on Midsummer's Eve. During the day, they collected herbs, flowers, and greenery to make flower crowns and to decorate the maypole.

A maypole was a long pole that had been painted green or white, wrapped in several colorful ribbons, and then decorated with flowers. It was then raised in a very green and open area, such as a garden or a field, and then the people danced around it to commemorate midsummer.

The evening itself was a huge event with many people gathering together to party, feast, eat, drink, and dance. The evening had a special significance when it came to romance. If a woman put flowers under her pillows on this evening, she'd get visions and dreams of her future husband.

Swedes ate traditional Swedish dishes like herring, potatoes, and lutefisk on this holiday. Speaking more on this subject, there were also loads of aquavit (a distilled spirit native to Scandinavia), grilled fish and meat roasts. For dessert, people ate lots of strawberries with cream.

A dish made from fermenting herring called Surstromming has a very pungent flavor and smell, and midsummer is considered incomplete without it. During the celebrations, people gathered around the table with their family and friends and used surstromming as the main dish for dinner. Of course, it came with sides of sour cream, chopped onions, boiled potatoes, and crisp bread.

HOW I CAN CELEBRATE MIDSUMMER

As a Norse Pagan, now is your time to make your festivities public and let it be known that you're going to uphold ancient traditions. Today, you can add your own dash of fun to things by making midsummer celebrations unique. Of course, you are expected to go outdoors and celebrate with traditional foods and drinks, do flower wreaths, and light bonfires, but you can do it all by adding your flair to things.

Go out!

The Swedes used to run to the hills and pastures during midsummer. So should you. Any green place would work, really, as long as you can be there and be festive. The subtler intent behind the meadow frolicking and pasture dancing is a deep appreciation for the bounties of summer.

Greenery, free-flowing water, blue skies, and the resplendent sun—these are all hallmarks of summer and a time when the Norse used to make the most out of this weather by harvesting, farming, and tilling the soil.

It doesn't just have to be some public green place; you can book a summer cottage, go out into the woods, or camp by a placid lake. Remember, it's all about leaving your unique footprint on the celebration.

Berries and Cream

While, okay, yes, for the more pedantic of my readers, I acknowledge the fact that strawberries technically belong to the banana family, but for the sake of the celebration, we're still going to count them as berries. Besides, there are also blueberries, mulberries, cherries, and all sorts of other fruits that exist in the legitimate berry family that you can include in your feasting.

And this is a day for traditional feasting. A day where pickled herring, salmon, vodka, schnapps, and healthy servings of potatoes and onions are supposed to entice you and then assuage your hunger.

Make use of the internet's rich reserves of recipes to make strawberry shakes, smoothies, cakes, and desserts. You can combine going out and feasting by taking some of your friends and family out for a picnic, complete with a checkered cloth and a big picnic basket.

Don't Forget the Flower Crowns

One of the more quintessential of midsummer celebrations are the flower crowns that are made from wildflowers found in summer fields. If you can, be very liberal with the flowers. Put 'em in vases, hang 'em in the maypole, make wreaths out of them, and of course, the flower crowns. And then dance with the scent of those flowers intoxicating you, giving you a natural high. Feel the nature all around you, on top of your head, and under your feet as you try to envision how the old Norse must have felt during this time. It's one of the ways you can be close to your ancestors during midsummer.

Mark the Occasion with a Bonfire

No midsummer would be complete without a bonfire, a bonfire specifically for the purpose of keeping the light going even at nighttime and for drawing away all the horrors, dark forces, and evil entities in the area.

If you're living in the American Midwest or Scandinavia, midsummer might be an excellent time for you to find a midsummer festival going on in your vicinity. They raise the midsummer pole, dance to traditional Scandinavian music, and make collective wreaths. Most modern-day festivals also offer meals, lodging, and plenty of activities throughout the entire day.

CHAPTER 9
FREYFAXI

Freyr was one of the most revered of the Norse gods. Originally a Vanir god, he was sent to Asgard after the Æsir-Vanir war and lived there with his sister and father. He later became the ruler of Alfheim, the home of the elves.

As the god of fertility and peace, he was linked to a good harvest, sunshine, the weather, favorable wind, prosperity, and male virility. Of his many responsibilities was to provide abundance, joy, good weather, great harvest, reward hard work, and give courage where courage was needed.

He could control the weather, especially the rain and the sun. He'd come to the help of those who needed his aid when it came to growing their crops.

But that did not mean that Freyr's expertise and godhood were limited to just agriculture. He was a major god, along the ranks of Odin and Frigg, and Thor.

THE CELEBRATION OF FREYFAXI

Also called Freysblót, the celebration behind this day is supposed to be an introspective one, calling to mind the fact that even though most of us do not practice farming ourselves, we still rely upon it just as our ancestors did thousands of years ago. We still eat the food that the farmers grow; it's just now we get it from farmer's markets, the grocery store, and supermarts. But we must not lose sight of who is responsible for these bounties.

It's Freyr, god of the sun and rain and harvests. The Norse folk thanked him for his gifts at Freyfaxi. And just as they did then, so should we now because without Freyr's light shining upon us, we wouldn't be able to get food.

Celebrated at the end of July or at the start of August, it falls in line with Lammas.

Historically, people used to celebrate this day by baking phallic-shaped bread to honor Freyr. It wasn't all phallic shaped, even though the phallus is one of Freyr's symbols, what with him being the god of male virility.

VENERATING FREYR

In terms of temperament, Freyr's more of a calm and cool god. He's easy to work with and venerate. It's almost second nature for him to come down and help those who direly need his aid in terms of farming, agriculture, and harvesting. But that is not the entire scope of his help.

Today, on Freyfaxi, you can venerate him for any number of reasons:

- If you're a parent, you can thank and venerate Freyr for making you a parent. As the god of male fertility, Freyr's responsible for ensuring that people get blessed with children. Well, it's a joint effort between him and Freya, his sister.
- If you're a landowner and use that land to grow crops.
- If you've particularly enjoyed the summer and spring seasons this year. Freyr's responsible for that in large part, as he controls the rain, the sunshine, and the wind.

When making an offering to him, you can place baked bread on the altar. The ingredients of this bread must be as natural and organic as possible, as Freyr's kind of a stickler for that. Any locally grown or organic food would be excellent as an offering to him. If it's a meal that you're offering as a sacrifice, make it a homely, nice meal that comes from humane and ethical sources.

Freyr loves his beer and cherries. Consider offering him a local craft beer and a bowl of cherries with a side of bread.

It doesn't just have to be food. You can offer him clothing. He's fond of linen—it being a plant fiber—and cotton. Freyr's favorite colors are golden, green, and yellow. He used to wear this special crown made from wheat, barley, and leaves. If you make that, you'll have his attention for sure.

He was not big on hostility, so offering him any weapons —even something as trivial as a belt knife—would not be wise. While other gods might appreciate weapons— Odin, Thor, Heimdall, to name a few—Freyr does not want any sort of weapons as offerings or in the vicinity of his blót.

One special sign that Freyr's going to send you, especially if you've called onto him and are in need of his help, is he's going to blow on your chest or forehead. You'll feel a gentle wind there. This, according to him, is called blowing his light into you. Afterward, if you concentrate, you'll feel a coolness coming off from where he blew into you.

A simple Freyfaxi ceremony can include the following:

1. A sacred space
2. Some attendees for the event
3. Venerating Freyr by reading Skaldic poetry
4. Filling a horn with mead and passing it around while toasting Freyr and asking for his blessings
5. Hailing Freyr and emptying the libation for the local spirits

Begin by setting up a space that you've consecrated for the blót. Welcome everyone who's attending and have them seated around a circle. Then explain the purpose of the blót out loud.

"Today, we're here to honor and venerate the Norse god, Freyr, the lord of Alheim, a chief Vanir."

Pass around the horn of mead to everyone attending, and then have each of them toast him by saying, "Hail Freyr, god of sunshine, god of rain, god of the summer harvest. Bless us with your abundance, Lord of Alfheim. Bless us with your prosperity, O' wise and generous Freyr. Hail Freyr!"

If anyone has any offerings to make for Freyr, they can place them at the helm of the sacred space, where you can place a makeshift altar. Once the horn of mead has made a complete circle, hail Freyr one last time and then pour the libation out in the open.

In doing so, you'll have pleased Freyr and will have ensured that the god of fertility bestows his blessings on you and the attendees of the blót.

CHAPTER 10
HAUSTBLÓT

Around the 20th to 23rd of September, the Norse pagans used to celebrate the autumn equinox, also called the Haustblót. It was a time for them to anticipate the shortening of days as the winter neared. For the next six months, winter's hold would be long, fierce, and dark. At this time, the crops were coming to an end, and those in charge of harvesting them were starting to gather and preserve them for the long winter ahead.

At this time, in the autumnal season, the world became red and colorful, with various shades of red, orange, and yellow, everywhere as far as the eye could see. Some likened it to blood, others likened it to fire. At this time, the animals started to hibernate and birds migrated to warmer locations. Ravens would be seen flying across the horizon, seeking carrion.

For the Norse folk, this was a time to give thanks to the gods and goddesses of fertility for the bounties they had gifted in the summer. These bounties would see them through the winter. It was also a time to pray to the gods, the spirits of the land, nature, and the ancestors to look over the people, to give them courage, and to keep their hearts and hearths warm in the winter. The Norse folk believed in elves—as we've seen in Alfablót—and they considered these elves powerful beings who could turn the lands fertile if they wished. This was a time for the people to pray to the elves so that they'd maintain the lands during the winter so that they'd be fertile in the upcoming summer.

Haustblót was also known as the fall feast or Winter Finding. Remember the three sacrifices that Odin mentioned? One at the beginning of winter, one in the middle of winter, and the third in the summer? We've already covered the latter two. Haustblót was the one at the start of winter.

Besides the blót, people used to celebrate it with bonfires, singing, dancing, feasting, and bidding the summers goodbye. It was also time for the people to start gathering their livestock, such as their sheep, and round them up.

Every autumn task that had to be done was done around this time—gathering and storing wood for the fires, making sure that all the ships were tied and moored, ensuring that all the enclosures around the farmsteads were secure, checking on the food reserves to see if they'd last through the winter, doing necessary repairs around the house, making everything winter-proof, and preparing winter clothes for everyone in the house.

The two main deities who were venerated during this blót were Freyr—because he's the god of sunshine, prosperity, rain, and fertility—and Skadi—the goddess of winter, hunting, and frost.

HOW YOU CAN CELEBRATE

Bonfires, dancing, and feasting aside, this is a great time to start taking care of your pets. If you have dogs that are winter-sensitive, it's time to arrange indoor heating for them. The same goes for cats and parrots, especially if you're living in an area that gets affected by winter. Make sure that your animal family is in good health. It might be an excellent time to take them to a vet for their yearly checkup.

For some reason, it's just hard for me to picture barbequing in the summer. The heat of the grill and the whole hassle of having to maintain it in scorching temperatures is something that I'll never get. But come fall, especially on those crisp and cool nights, there's nothing better than a family barbeque. Just so we're on the same page, the family gets together for the barbeque, it's not the family that gets barbequed. And for Haustblót, I see no better reason than to take that grill out, light up the bonfire pit, and gather the family around for a nice barbecue.

If that's not your speed, then why not try your hand at a seasonal feast? Fall foods like squashes, nuts, root veggies, and apples can make one heck of a mean salad. It's a great time for foraging for wild edibles like pawpaws, walnuts, and crab apples. And since it's the fall, you can do with a plump pumpkin too.

While supermarkets and grocery stores have made the entire point of storing food redundant, there's still some traditional satisfaction to be had in going old-fashioned and canning your food, fermenting it, dehydrating it, and freezing it, especially if you want to keep true to the haust-blót theme.

The old Norse pagans used this celebration as a time to be introspective, thoughtful, and grateful. They thanked each other, the gods, and their ancestors for everything that they'd reaped during the summer. We can continue that tradition and be thankful for our prosperity, wealth, and happiness.

It's also a reminder to us that our ancestors, with sheer perseverance, hard work, and patience, harvested the land and reaped the rewards of their hard work. It's a testament to the fact that no effort goes wasted. If we can put this thought into daily practice, it can boost our morale and provide us with hope and courage. Hope and courage that we all need sometimes.

Now's your last chance to get in all the fall colors before the winter. A solitary or group hike might be an excellent opportunity to get all those fall sights in. Take a few hours out of your day today and indulge in all the colors that nature has to offer.

Lastly, as this is a blót, do not forget the chief gods and goddesses to venerate at an altar this time of the year. The ones at the top of your list should be Freyr, Gerðr, Freyja, Thor, Sif, Odin, Freya, and Skadi.

CHAPTER 11
VETRNÆTR

Cyclicality had been hardwired into the ethos of the Norse folk. It was a somewhat harsh concept that they had all come to terms with, whether it was in the form of Ragnarök (the destruction of the world and the death of the gods, followed by the rebirth of the world) or their daily lives (where they had to strive through the summers to be able to endure the winters), and in doing so had created a rich celebratory culture that propped it up.

End of the winter? That sounds like the best time for a feast and some merriment.

End of the summer? Oh well, we did as best as we could, and now it's time to reap the rewards of our hard work through some lively celebration.

WHAT IS VETRNÆTR?

It was in this similar vein that Winter Nights or Vetrnætr was celebrated. It held a significant position among their annual celebrations. Observed at the end of the summer and at the cusp of winter, Vetrnætr was one of the most mentioned celebrations in the old sagas. In fact, in the Ynlingsaga, it is mentioned alongside Jólablót—also known as Yule—and Sigrblót—which was the victory sacrifice at the start of each summer.

If you're wondering when Vetrnætr begins this year, it's on October 28th, 2023. It is said to occur on the first full moon of October. This was how the old Norse people kept track of time, by assigning it relativity to the moon. In this way, Vetrnætr was also said to be celebrated three full moons before Yule. Each new moon was the start of a new month for the Norse people, and some appearances of the moon were celebrated, such as Vetrnætr.

While Winter Nights were celebrated for many reasons, one of the main reasons for observing this celebration was the Wild Hunt. If you have read the Witcher books, played its games, or watched the TV show, you might have heard of the Wild Hunt. The Wild Hunt was this great, phantasmal nocturnal horde that stampeded across the night sky. It was also called Odin's Hunt or Terrifying Ride.

Some said that if the horde—that prowled through the wilderness—came across a person, or if a person was unlucky enough to look up to the night sky while the Hunt was on the prowl, they'd take that person's soul to Hel. It was said that the first frost of the year was left in the wake of the Hunt, letting people know that the horde has passed for the time being and also serving as a cause for celebration.

Other prominent reasons to celebrate this holiday included thanking the gods for a successful harvest and asking for their protection from the toils of winter. As hardy as the Norse folk were, they knew that they had to take the winters seriously. This celebration was done more in that vein than any other.

According to some sources, Winterfylleth, Haustblót, Disablót, and Winter Nights are just different names for Vetrnætr.

WHEN TO CELEBRATE IT?

Winter nights were celebrated in Gormánuður. It was a three-day affair that began on the first full moon after the first proper frost. Besides being a lunisolar calendar, the Norse calendar also relied upon weather patterns, which is why the exact timing of this celebration was not absolute. Later on, though, when the Viking Age arrived in 800-1000 CE, people began to celebrate Winter nights on a set date.

On modern calendars, the celebration lands between the 19th and 26th of October. According to historian Andreas Nordberg, major holidays, blóts, and sacrifices were held 28 days after an equinox or solstice, as we discussed in the previous chapter. This meant that the Winter nights took place roughly 28 days after the Autumnal equinox.

WAS IT JUST THE NORSE WHO CELEBRATED WINTER NIGHTS?

The Norse Sagas have clear and frequent mention of Winter nights. Therefore, it's safe to say that Winter nights fall within the Norse pagan branch of heathenism. Other celebrations that line up with Winter nights include Samhain, which is considered to be the origin of

Halloween. As Winter Nights is a Norse celebration, Samhain is a Gaelic one and is observed by modern-day Wiccans, Celts, Irish, and Scottish people.

Coming back to Winter nights, today, most Scandinavian organizations celebrate it and consider it a festival. All over the world, wherever there are Norse Pagans—such as in North America, Canada, United Kingdom, Winter nights are observed. Within Norse Paganism, communities like Ásatrú and Vanatru observe this celebration as it pertains to both the Æsir gods and the Vanir ones. Frey was honored during Winter nights as well as Odin, Skadi, and Ullr. Sometimes, even good old Thor was thrown into the mix.

For modern paganists, the Winter Nights have held the significance of being one of the primary festivals that also happens to be true to the lore, meaning it hasn't been reinvented or shaped in the past century. Even though our modern calendar has shifted so drastically, Vetrnætr still marks a pivoting point in the year when the sun and warmth finally retire and make way for the cold and dark.

As modern-day Norse Pagans, it falls on us to uphold the traditions of our ancestors, spiritual or otherwise.

HOW CAN I CELEBRATE VETRNÆTR?

Keep it simple

Unlike the bigger holidays like Yule, Vetrnætr does not require as much planning or preparation. This holiday comes at very short notice. More importantly, it's about spending time with your loved ones in the comfort of your warm home, gathered around a fireplace, welcoming the change in weather with songs, drinks, food, and laughter. It's a way to remind us that the coldest and darkest months can have the warmest and lightest moments.

Be generous

Speaking of which, one other purpose of Vetrnætr was to help people cope with the anticipatory anxiety of the upcoming challenges of winter. Nowadays, even though we have departmental stores, marts, and shops that have everything available year-round, this celebration can serve as a great reminder that the Norse folk found courage in each other's company despite the scarcity of resources. Perhaps that's what we need sometimes too. It can also be a time when we become more mindful of those in the world who face shortages of food, water, and resources.

In that spirit, you can donate to your local shelter, soup kitchen, and charity organizations.

Feast with your family

You can invite your closest friends and family members for a dinner where you can perform a ritual blót and sumbel. Doing so can help you reconnect with your faith and assert the significance of the gods and goddesses, especially at this time of the year.

Welcome your forebears

Your ancestors are a part of you. This concept is seen in the Norse concept of soul. The Norse believed in a multi-faceted soul, with each part heading in different directions after a person's death. Our ancestors, through one of the facets of their souls, live within us.

When you gather around with your friends and family for the feast, invoke your ancestors, remember them, and welcome their spirit to the feast. You may remember them by sharing their life stories, discussing their acts of valor and honor, and talking about how they were in life.

Sumbel

A sumbel is a ritual wherein you make toasts to deities, your ancestors, and to the heroes of yore while drinking from a shared horn filled with an alcoholic drink, preferably mead or ale. Additionally, as is common during a sumbel, the last round of drinking comes with making oaths. As this is just the start of winter, now might be an excellent time to take some oaths.

Blót

You can honor the gods by symbolically offering food and drink to them. You can perform a blót by casting your offerings into a fire or by placing them at an altar.

The four gods that you should remember at this time, specifically for the blót and sumbel, are Freyr, Odin, Skadi, and Ullr.

Back in the old days, they used to offer meat as an offering to the gods, which made sense since a lot of the meat could not be stored for the winter. Meat, along with ale and mead, were the prominent offerings during the blóts historically.

Say a prayer

During these celebrations, the Norse folk used to say, "Til árs ok friðar!" which meant "to a good year and peace."

You can say this prayer with your friends and family, and add some more festivity to it, such as:

"To my friends and family,

May your bellies be full with warm food,

May your cups ever remain filled with good drinks,

May your kin and kith be safe from all harm and danger,

May your crops (businesses, endeavors, careers, etc.) grow,

May you prosper in every endeavor you partake in,

May your door be open to those less fortunate than you,

May your skills remain sharp and your senses agile,

May we all now feast as if we had Sæhrímnir in our hall and Heiðrun on our roofs!"

CHAPTER 12
ÁLFABLÓT

Álfablót, meaning ritual for the elves, was a sacrificial celebration that was shrouded in secrecy. Its significance has been attested in historical texts such as the Austrfararvísur. An excerpt from the text is as follows:

> "'Do not come any farther in, wretched fellow', said the woman; 'I fear the wrath of Óðinn; we are heathen.' The disagreeable female, who drove me away like a wolf without hesitation, said they were holding a sacrifice to the elves inside her farmhouse."

It is from this passage alone that it is clear that Álfablót was a secretive affair, unlike most communal Germanic celebrations.

The elves were thought to be these godly beings, possessing abilities like magic, grace, and splendor. They could interfere in the affairs of humans and make someone's health better or worse, depending upon that person's standing with the elves. The elves had their own realm called Alfheim, of whom the god Freyr was the ruler, along with his wife, Gerd.

This year, Álfablót will be celebrated on the 28th of October 2023 or the 27th of November during the full moon.

WHAT WAS ÁLFABLÓT?

Strangers were warded off at this time of celebration, and only those who belonged to the household could partake in this indoor ritual. Considering that most Norse rituals, in some way or other utilized the outdoors for their processions, the Álfablót was quite distinct in terms of this aloofness.

Even though there is not enough to go on, it's been gathered from resources and historians that animals were sacrificed, and their blood was poured on a cairn or a hilltop. The meat could have either been left for the elves as tribute or eaten by the people as part of a feast to honor the Alfheim residents.

One particular historical account from 14th-century Norway states that women used to bring food to caves and cairns and then consecrated it to the elves and then ate it later on. Just as offering food was considered important for this ritual, so was beer. Some men were designated as beer men, who had the role of providing beer as well as drinking copious amounts of it.

From here, we can infer that Álfablót involved sacrificing animals, followed by a feast and drinking. It is also suggested that since this was near the time of the Wild Hunt's appearance, there was an air of fear around this celebration. Perhaps that's why it was celebrated so furtively.

WHY WAS IT CELEBRATED?

This was a day to honor one's ancestors and other beings like elves and spirits of the land. In some accounts, it is believed that after a person died, in a specific case, they'd transcend into an elf. This was one of the many possibilities for those who had died. They could go to Valhalla, Folkvangr, Hel, linger as a spirit on earth, or, in this case, become an elf.

So, people had two causes to celebrate this day. Firstly, they could implore the elves to grant them favors. As mentioned before, the elves had almost godlike magical powers that they could use to bring about good health, luck, and prosperity to a person. Inversely, they could also bring bad luck and bad health to someone. Was it perhaps that the people were afraid of the elves' wrath that there was an air of fear around this celebration?

Other gods were worshipped and venerated during Álfablót, too, including Freyr.

The Norse folk believed that they were not alone in the world. Besides the gods, goddesses, animals, and plants, they believed that the world around them was filled with mystical creatures like sprites, supernatural entities, dwarves, trolls, huldras, and elves. Elves, the Norse people believed, could impart wisdom, guidance, and magical aid.

The people who celebrated Álfablót wanted to build a relationship with the spirits around them, particularly those of the elves, believing that these spirits were linked to the fertility of the land (a recurring theme for this time of the year) and their ancestors as well. It was a very exclusive time, one where strangers were not allowed near the farmsteads.

HOW WAS IT CELEBRATED?

You'd be surprised to know that this ceremony, quaint and secluded as it was, was initiated and administrated by the woman of the household.

Since this was a blót, like most blóts, it had three major parts—the consecration of the offering, the sharing of the offering, and the libation. In the past, the offering was an animal. For modern practice, you can either make do with food or meats that you sourced from a store strictly for the purpose of sacrificial offering. You can also make do with mead and beer and skip the meat entirely.

The first step was consecrating the offering, the leader of the ritual would offer the sacrifice to the elves, ancestors, and gods, and then sacrifice the animal. They'd then spill its blood on the ground. The remaining parts of the offering were served as a feast, the drinks as a libation, and then, after remembering the ancestors, elves, and gods, the ceremony would come to a close with a prayer.

HOW CAN I CELEBRATE IT?

Remember the intent behind Álfablót. It's to remember your ancestors and to get back in touch with the spirits of the land. You can take your cue from how Álfablót was celebrated by the old Norse people and choose to host a dinner just for your family. It's at this dinner that your family members can gather and drink toasts to the deceased members of your family and honor them by sharing their stories.

This can also be done after dinner, in your backyard, or around a bonfire.

Of course, if you have offerings, you can leave them by a makeshift mound, altar, or out in nature. Spirits and animals can come to find that offering easily.

CHAPTER 13

THANK YOU FOR LETTING ME BE YOUR GUIDE THROUGH THE NORSE HOLIDAYS

I'm sure you're wondering how you can help others experience the same joy and fulfillment you have gained from reading this book.

Leaving a review can be a great way. Your review can help people discover the book and provide an opportunity to share your experience and what you've learned on your journey.

To leave a review, scan the QR code above OR type http://amazon.com/review/create-review?&asin=B0C67T6W66

AFTERWORD

While I have tried to present to you as many Norse Pagan holidays as I could, I will admit that this list is not exhaustive. Truth is, there's no list out there that's completely exhaustive. So much of our history has been lost. We have the sagas and the historical texts to guide us in the right direction, but even then, there's no telling how many other holidays and celebrations the Norsemen used to celebrate that have not made their way to us through history.

Some of them have been tarnished by Christianization, morphed and disfigured from their original roots. Take Yule, Easter, Midsummer, and Freyfaxi for instance. It is because of the hard work of many pagans that we still have an understanding of the underlying real holidays and traditions that existed more than a thousand years ago.

But just as I have cautioned you right now, I must also give you good tidings. The good news is that the gods have not abandoned us. The mere fact that paganism and heathenry have been revived after all this time, its rituals, traditions, and celebrations being recreated by devoted pagans all over the world is proof that the Norse gods are still there and they still care about people like you and me. Our efforts, our observance of the festivities, they're not wasted. Trust me. The gods and goddesses witness us, and when our need is dire, they come to aid us.

We must hold on to the hope that just as all of the current paganism has made its way back to us, so will more of it through the help of the gods. My effort to bring these celebrations to you and your efforts to read them and learn more about paganism can be likened to Odin's quest to unearth great mysteries. It was in search of these mysteries that he lost his eye. That he wedged his spear in his side and hung from the Yggdrasil for nine days and nine nights, bleeding out. He came out on the other side with the wisdom of runes, with the knowledge of fate and magic, and just like him, we're coming out on the other side with knowledge of ancient magical traditions.

I intended to share with you the Norse calendar and the major holidays through this book, and I feel like I have done that. Let's do a summary of everything we've learned in this book.

- In the beginning, we went over the Norse months of the year, the characteristics of the lunisolar Norse calendar, and what each month denoted. With an understanding of the agricultural and summer/winter polarized calendar of the Norse folk, we moved on to the major celebrations that they observed throughout the year.

- We began with Winter Nights and learned how the arrival of winter foretold a time of hardship for the Norse folk.
- In a similar spirit, we learned about Álfablót and how it was a time to venerate one's ancestors and the Alfheim elves.
- Next, we saw how the Norse people observed Þorrablót, a time when people bolstered each other's spirits to endure the rest of the winter.
- We also took a look at the Norse men's and women's day, Bóndadagur and Konudagur, and how both of them were celebrated.
- Moving on, we saw one of the important celebrations, Sígrblót, or the victory celebration that heralded the arrival of summer.
- Speaking of summer, we discussed the Nordic origins and celebrations of Midsummer, and what sort of cuisine was preferable at that time, along with the importance of flowers and green magic.
- We went over Yule and saw how this once Pagan celebration had been morphed into modern-day Christmas. In this critical chapter, I filtered out the original Pagan holiday, giving you the authentic experience of how Yule used to be celebrated.
- Then we learned about Disablót, a time to venerate the Dísir and female deities.
- The second last chapter was about Haustblót, a time to give thanks for the harvest and get ready for the winter by winding up one's autumnal tasks.
- Lastly, we saw how Freyfaxi or Freysblót was a time to venerate the god of sunshine, rain, harvest, and fertility.

And now, I am confident that you have the framework for the annual celebrations that the old Norse Pagans used to observe, that many modern-day neo-pagan organizations like Ásatrú observe to this day. Some of these are holidays and celebrations that are still being celebrated in Scandinavian countries, such as Midsummer.

The purpose of sharing insights about these celebrations was to instill a deeper appreciation for the old Norse culture that still lives on to this day in our hearts and in our practice. Equipped with this information, you can become the most authentic pagan version of yourself.

If you liked this book, I have two others that are all about Norse Mythology and Norse Magic. Please do check them out on my Amazon author's page to learn more about the Norse gods and goddesses, the Vikings, the history of the Norse folk, and how you can become a practitioner of Norse magic by utilizing runes—and so much more!

I'd love for you to share your feedback with me and rate this book on Amazon so that other readers who are looking for helpful stuff about Norse mythology can find their way to this book.

I am deeply grateful to you for reading and reviewing this book and for striving to become a better pagan.

Sjáumst sienna!

RESOURCES

1. Amajarl. (2022, January 20). Álfablót - The forgotten rite of ancestor worship. https://draugablikk.com/myth-mankind/alfablot-the-forgotten-rite-of-ancestor-worship/

2. Fornkunskap. (2014, October 1). Vetrnætr. https://fornkunskap.wordpress.com/2014/10/01/vetrnaetr/

3. Furstenau, S. O. (2022, January 1). The Old Norse calendar. https://www.icelandicroots.com/post/the-old-norse-calendar

4. Hartman, J. (2022, October 13). Vetrnætr for the family. https://www.pagankids.org/post/vetrn%C3%A6tr

5. Nomads, T. (2021, October 8). *The Norse Wheel of the year: The norse calendar & holidays*. Time Nomads | Your Pagan Store Online. https://www.timenomads.com/the-norse-wheel-of-the-year-viking-calendar-holidays/

6. Quickbutik. (n.d.). Álfablót - old norse Halloween - soldiser - norse jewelry & accessories. https://soldiser.com/pages/alfablot-old-norse-halloween

7. Rummel, R. (2018, September 6). *Iceland's Thorrablot Festival keeps Viking Cuisine alive*. Atlas Obscura. https://www.atlasobscura.com/foods/thorrablot-midwinter-festival-iceland

8. *Þorrablót*. Guide to Iceland. (n.d.). https://guidetoiceland.is/connect-with-locals/sigrunthormar/orrablot

9. Wikimedia Foundation. (2023, February 19). *Man's day and woman's day (Iceland)*. Wikipedia. https://en.wikipedia.org/wiki/Man%27s_Day_and_Woman%27s_Day_(Iceland)

10. Arithharger. (2017, March 21). *Sígrblót – the victory blessing*. Whispers of Yggdrasil. https://arithharger.wordpress.com/2017/03/21/sigrblot-the-victory-blessing/

11. Norman, R. T. (2023, May 21). *What are all of the Scandinavian midsummer traditions?*. Scandinavia Standard. https://www.scandinaviastandard.com/what-are-all-of-the-scandinavian-midsummer-traditions/

12. Viking Dragon / Jelling Dragon. (2021, December 13). *The origins of yule*. Viking Dragon / Jelling Dragon. https://thevikingdragon.com/blogs/news/the-origins-of-yule

13. Bernott, K. (2023, February 1). *What is Dísablót?*. SHIELDMAIDEN'S SANCTUM. http://www.shieldmaidenssanctum.com/blog/2023/2/1/what-is-disablot

14. Vanorio, A. (2022, September 5). *Haustblot: Norse Fall Feast*. Celebrate Pagan Holidays. https://www.celebratepaganholidays.com/fall/haustblot-norse-fall-feast

15. *Freyfaxi: The-Ásatrú-community*. the. (n.d.). https://www.theÁsatrúcommunity.org/freyfaxi